Dedication

To the Broken Guitar and Heartstrings.

Let Us Sing.

Hey There, John Mayer

I love the way your hand trembles when

There is discord among chords

I love the way your voice trembles when

There is trouble among treble

I recognize your obsession with perfection

In my flawed reflection

We are not these insecurities

Let us see the purity in the impurities

Let us be worry free of worry, we--

We are me

We are the heart of me

We are the thought of me

Room for Squares

No Such Thing

Grateful that you can see the phoenix in my ruins
Grateful for he who can be magic among humans
And if this is but an alluring illusion--
I am grateful to be blinded by your lumens

Why Georgia

Me: Why do you hold it all in?

Him: Good question.

My Stupid Mouth

Equilibrium could be
Considered a state of stagnancy
And then would we
Consider it our agony?
Nothing ever changes-- same shit different days
Has us rearranging the pieces to excite the being
Delight the being
Fight the being
Bite the being
Are our souls feeding
Or our egos eating
Are we being?
Unnecessarily needy

Your Body is a Wonderland

It's the rainbow in the iris of your kaleidoscope eyes
Like a rainstorm of riddles falling from the skies
It's the way you hold your hands
Tranquilly across your thighs
The delicacy of your fingers as they intertwine
I can't help but wonder
What they would feel like between mine
Longing for the potency of finger-tracing spines
And the moment your lips
Will finally interrupt my rhymes

Neon

Like a mime
Painted white
Blank expression
Lost in time
Lack of might
False objections
Still confined
Spiraled flight
Dark projections
Walk the line
Out of sight
Black reflection

City Love

Countless stares of deep despair
Etched upon the concrete stairs—
Where a haven has been paved
Between blades of green shades
And the daintily dancing wind
But unlike them, I lift my chin
I twirl and spin in Earth's hair
Feeling as free as my feet bare

83

Baby

I'm a thinker

Not a screamer

Hook

Line

And

Sinker:

I'm a dreamer

3x5

I stare and I wonder
I worry and I fumble
I stare and I wonder

I frown and I ask
I assume and I attack
I frown and I ask

I smile and I wait
I hope and I pray
I smile and I wait

Love Song for No One

Nothing raises the hair on my neck like when
I'm pressing your pages with my pen
When you touch me, I moan out
And mentally roam out
And take a loan out of you
And when we reach the climax, I conceive
My nipples raised to receive
The sweet nectar of life that keeps us alive
After night after night of deceit
Nature and nurture
I hate you
It's torture
You are all that I need
I love you

Back to You (ft. Ambien)

Now I lay me down to sleep
Smoked some good weed not to think
About the life out in those streets
Mind's at ease between these sheets
I'm racing down the road tonight
Gazing through the amber light
Think I might stop and get a Sprite
Slowing down, it's on my right
Or did I pass it just a slight?
Turn around, I think I might
I should really check my sight
Back to you my shining knight
How did I get up on this kite?
I'll be sure, I meant, alright

Great Indoors

Eye for eye

A soul for a soul

One day you will see

I was as true as I spoke it

And if you do unto others

As you'd like done unto you

The sick and the poor

Would be the far

And the few

Not Myself

We are bags of bones
In temporary homes
Adams of atoms
And cleaves of Eves
But some of us are prophecies
Muhammad, Gandhi, Dalai Lama
However that you want it
Universe calls it karma
Universal law, it's dharma
Plant a seed, pollination bees
Feed the need in the garden
Eat an apple down in Eden
The hell that we be in
Is partly what we needed

St. Patrick's Day

If he were just a dream, he wouldn't have left a bruise when my heart he tightly squeezed, licked his fingers, winked his eye, and watched me fall to my knees. He raped my mouth, no words came out, just eyes screaming please. Heart's racing, mind's chasing the reason he's doing this to me. What shall be, will be, it all ends fatally. But if he lived life more than theatrically, maybe miraculously he would find what he's been searching for. Models in his bed. He still wants more. Lines in his head. His body on the floor. He's the walking dead-- has that zombie man allure. He can't feel me, he can't feel me-- I'm trying to touch his core, take off his armor, disarm him-- has that Sir Lancelot couture. And I don't mean no harm, no, I don't mean no pain. Please understand I'm trying to cleanse him through this rain. And when he sees the rainbow, true beauty he will then know.

I was his pot of gold.

Heavier Things

Clarity

Even though we assume
We can naturally see
We need ego casualty
Truths misconstrued and misused
Leaves us confused and contused
We need clarity
To speak how we feel
To speak on our real
And not hide ourself mentally

Bigger Than My Body

Your words are
Like fingertips
That trace my hips
In the still of the night
Your words are like eyes
That watch my chest
As it falls and it rises
And falls

Something's Missing

I stared at the only truth I've known
On her death bed in August of '08
And the last time I told her I loved her
I cried it to her because I was too late
Sometimes I see her in my dream state
Bringing backwards omens to translate
Leading me to the lighter
To raise my spirit higher
When I can't decipher
I just need some light
Some hindsight
Some insight
Something

New Deep

I want to sit atop a billboard beneath the twilight
Studying your facade filtered by the moonlight
And the alteration of display affected by the spotlight
The irony of the epitome of an authentic light zeitgeist
Professing an existence benighted under midnight

Come Back to Bed

Lying here next to your shirt again
Because it's hard to accept the end
Something about the smell of the nape
Of your neck after eighteen hours of day
As we lie side by side to try to derive
The direction of life before death
Before our thoughts are dismantled
With each deeper breath
Before realizing we are now chest to chest
Our hearts beat in sync, we are clinching our teeth
And grasping each other
As our shoulders slip under the covers
We start to fade from friendship to lovers
As we toss and turn each other
Lost in hugs and rubs and smothered
By the flames ignited until we came and tried to hide it
We divided love

Home Life

Something about that moment when
You put your arm around my waist and
Pull me in at five in the morning
Before the existential dread sets in
As my looming alarm dooms our zen
Sometimes that moment lasts all day
Sometimes that moment tends to stray
But within that moment, I'm okay

Split Screen Sadness

Him: Why do we long for people?

Me: I don't know. It could be hell if you think about it

Him: Maybe it's part of hell

Me: An inspired hell

Daughters (The Son Effect)

These broken boys break me
They mentally shake me
They fake like they date me
To emotionally rape me
These broken boys break me
But these boys don't make me
These boys make more boys
To perpetuate the cycle of breaking
Hearts
These boys and their poisonous darts
These boys are greatly underappreciating
Too busy sedating
The next girl's emotions to rape, see
It's not just me
These broken boys are breaking
Leaving children without fathers
Because you did not have one
Is not an excuse to not raise your sons
These broken boys are breaking families
Breaking traditions

Breaking sanities on broken expeditions
These broken boys are breaking
These broken boys aren't braking
These broken boys are breaking
And I don't know how to save me

Only Heart

He asked what inspires me and I said, "emotion."
I meant tragedy and love and all our commotion.

Wheel

I don't churn the wishing wheel
Watch me turn the fishing reel
In burgundy water that used to be teal
Third degree wine stains under my heels
Insurgency internally I was built to rebel
I won't face the silence encompassing hell
As the muted riots summon the seventh seal
Chess against the reaper as I make an appeal
To convince the people it's time that we heal

Continuum

Waiting on the World to Change

God, if You can hear me can You simply tell me why?
Can You wrap my mind around
The pink streaks in the sky?
I thought that space is blue
And the clouds- that they are white
But now I'm taken by the view
Wondering if You control my sight
Wondering if a select few get awaken in the night
Perhaps it's on Your cue, God
That I'm chosen for this fight
For others to learn through and
Maybe then they will see the light
That we wouldn't wish to redo
If at first we did what's right

I Don't Trust Myself (With Loving You)

I beg your fucking pardon?

Sculptures in my chest

And voodoo in my garden

Belief

I have felt the resting of my heart
I did not breathe therein my start
And when they meet therein my dark
Death is but a transcended spark

Gravity

I don't mean to buzzkill, but when he says lovely

He actually means fuck me

Oh, he says he loves you? That's funny--

He loved me

He loves you, too

He gets mushy

He gets it in

He's the master of getting pussy

It's like he fell into me

And I into he

Yes, yes, yes

The irony

The Heart of Life

Hey grey sky
I'm not scared of you
I kind of like the things you do
All of that yelling and tree-shaking
Hailing and soil-raping
Implant those seeds of life
What seems bad today will rock me to sleep tonight
And when I awaken to the morning's light
I'll go pick a berry and take a bite
Refreshing

Vultures

What can I say; I'm destined by a pattern

This, that, this, that

Diss that, miss that, want that back

I think I can, I think I can like Thomas on his track

But then they invented planes and Thomas was like, "Where they do that at?"

"Trusting the unbelievable

will conceive the unperceivable"

That's what I keep telling them

Not believing it myself because I'm not believing him

Because he's mastered the art of retrieving them

Deceiving me to receive me to leave me sad and

It takes two to tango so shit's got me itching

He throws me in the ditch

At the first glimpse of a glitching

Sucks up all my blood and

He's wondering why I'm twitching

Stop This Train
(An Ode to Andrea)

She is the light in every lightning strike
The force behind eternity
Majestic magnetic energy
Her alike
The inner me
Opalescent alchemy
Wanderlust internally
Like a train clash clad symphony
Lacking a certain serendipity
As if meant to be isn't meant for me
But the Universe still forcefully
Ignites

Slow Dancing in a Burning Room

Intertwined in the afterlife
Love offered me as sacrifice
Here dined by the antichrist
Wife of strife will not suffice
Fight the plight of freedom heist
Jesus Christ
Can you see him in my eyes?
Can you feel him in the skies?
Can you hear him in my whys?
His name is irrelevant
Only remember for the hell of it
To feel the fire of burning desire
Until the inspiration hits

Bold as Love

I love the way you play hard to get

Like when you asked why
I was playing hard to get
The fuck out of your car
I love you for who you are

Dreaming with a Broken Heart

Your heartbeat was my bedtime story.

In Repair

Has anyone seen him?
I don't know what he's done to me
Can anyone read him? Just give me a summary
To the man who sits in a blank stare
As if he doesn't care-- I see through you
Past the roots of your hair
I've touched your soul; I've taken you there
Golden is the day we find the rewind;
Golden is the day we can manipulate time and repair
Black is the day on which I walked away;
As black as the tunnel of the facial x-rays
Study my expression, pump me full of medicine
Because you didn't kill me--
Only my mentality and every speck of my reality
Really

I'm Gonna Find Another You

I am not sure when I morphed from sweet to shady
Almost as rotten as the apple the snake gave me
My Granny always said I would never be a lady
So I'm doing me, no more wasting time persuading
Hit him with a moral, leave him character debating
Tell him that I hate him, all my feelings rearranging
Tell him that I'm done, I cannot see him changing
Tell him that I'm leaving, he's constantly degrading
Tell him I cashed out, he has not been paying
Attention, can you hear me? I am not reiterating
I know you are busy talking, but hear what I am saying
When you were out with her, I too was out playing
More solid than steel was the pipe that he was laying

Battle Studies

Heartbreak Warfare

You are the wicked reason
I laugh at the word trust
Lives built on top of lies
Hearts beating in the dust
Your silence is but a guile
I know that you don't mean it
A fire burns behind my eyes
I know that you have seen it
A saccharine smoldering rise
That only you can extinguish

All We Ever Do is Say Goodbye

I'd be lying if I said I didn't miss you.

Read 5:01am

Half of my Heart

You remind me of art
I had once acquired
Gripped half of my heart
Amidst a raging fire
He elevated me higher
So close to the sun
We were bound to be burned
Scars of love learned
A reverberating hum
Of Universal desire

Who Says

Respect is no longer shown to the subjective
Adjectives are used to pursue hidden objectives
And time is just an imaginary line of made up numbers
Just like the words you use to hide up under

Perfectly Lonely

Sweet oblivion I'm living in

Speaking in metaphors and idioms

To idiots

Assassin

Him: I'll never kill you

I need you

Alive

Me: Oh. Is that so?

Him: Yes

Me: For what?

Him: Assisted homicides duh

Me: I'm burning my fingerprints off as we speak

Crossroads

Just like these childhood games we play
The days we spend laughing and running away
Are worth more than we give them value
The love we lose when we are just me and you
Just like these sunsets turn days
Wallowing in our soul's separate agonies
In remembrance, this song I sing
As we sit blankly staring and wondering
Red rover, red rover
Let's rewind time until last October
Red rover, red rover
Let's bob until the apple turns over

War of my Life

Have you ever wondered how some words can feel so heavy? Slicing up your heart like a word-mill of machetes. The pressure of the weight/wait when a lover is not ready. Linguistic warfare every word your mind's debating. End up like Em throwing up mom's spaghetti. Maybe she dropped some percs in it because her hand just can't stay steady. And everything you say is brushed off as simply petty. Might as well call me boopin' Betty-- Just a colorful creation of someone anti-masturbating. Situationally soul-negating. Supposed to love all, but I find myself hating. Hating humanity and hating everything. Hating myself for loving you so desperately. Asking myself what the fuck is wrong with me? Caught up on you so goddamn pathetically. I try to tell myself that it is just sympathy. We have a similar history. But I'm feeling more than empathetically. Wobbling off my axis, a lack of symmetry. Swerving off the road because I cannot see ahead of me and you refuse to move your hands from in front of my eyes. And I am tired of the wondering whys. I am tired of the lies. I am tired of the late-night cries. I am tired of this life.

Edge of Desire

I'm about to meet and greet her
She's got me feeling weaker
Seconds from a heart attack
Like Griffin, Peter
Got me filling up my sack
I just want to feed her
Eat her
Please her
Cream her
Lick her
Stick her
Dick her
And leave her

Do You Know Me

Because you
You could be the remedy
I see into you and you see into me
We harbor the same energies
The mental chains--
Insanity, conflict with identities, excessive vanity,
The mind games, misplaced blame
The same density and lack of common decency
We share a propensity, the same intensity
We are a common entity
But you see me as the enemy

Friends, Lovers, or Nothing

Get in where you fit in. Don't be the ditch they spit in. I'm never ever forgetting, but always reminiscing and when I feel like missing I remember when you dissed, and I can rhyme all day. Better believe I can glide all night. So, I don't need to beef up because I don't have to fight for it. It's my God given right to it. Trying to sing since Advent at age seven. Knew it wouldn't work out since around eleven. So, I picked up the pen because it wasn't Armageddon. In the game I had to get my head in. Make a beat with my feet as the streets I tread in. Countless demons I've beheaded and I'm only just beginning. The future I'm not dreading because I know where I'm heading and I don't need directions from Tom-Tom or his brethren. I'm resting in peace and I'm not even dead yet. Flying high in life is my Heaven. In loving memory, I am never disappearing. So, despite what you may hear friend, I'm here until the ending. 2022 or whatever you believe in. Keep tabs on me because I'm constantly achieving and even for no reason and during every season and if I ever get in trouble it will probably be for treason or smoking trees some place where it's illegal in. Even in a cell I would keep circling. The thoughts in your mind be about me all time. And even though you never said it-- I always knew it. Makes me mad you only seek me when you're going through it. And when I tell you I'm through with it you want to act a jackass. All your words have been retracted. Well here are mine. I'll let you have it or forfeit it. Baby, it's friends, lovers, or nothing and don't you again forget it.

Born and Raised

Queen of California

Promised a weekend at the Westin, no questions
Knew that he was selling dreams
Stash of big weapons, no questions
Things are never as they seem
L.A. men, L.A. men—
They always hit me up when they really need a friend
When they're high, when they're horny
Surrounded by model bitches and lonely
They taunt me, they lure me
Pretend that they adore me
Because they long for the girl
Who doesn't tour them for their money
It's funny, it's love
It's California, so it never was

The Age of Worry

Hidden within the sway of my feet
As I lie in the dark dreaming of sleep
Buried within my unsteady hands
As I try to understand all that I am

Shadow Days

What could have been
Should have been
Would have been

Didn't

That's what I tell myself when I catch her reminiscing

Tell her not to do it when she dreams about your kiss And
tell her not to do it when she thinks she's missing

I tell her to keep strong-- don't slip into remission

Let's cook up a cure-- I tell her slip into the kitchen

Ask her what is life but many a decision

Yea, I know he's beautiful, but sight another vision

Paint another picture

Maybe read some scripture

Practice memory omission and try to stop reliving

All the things that he didn't

Speak for Me

But here you are in the dark next to my beating heart

Offering silent reassurance that

You are not here to hurt me

You just don't want to get hurt, see

I see that

I feel like you need that

Silence

Something Like Olivia

If I was not at work
If I had time to think
I would fill up your mind
I would fill up the sink
Pressing your head until
You gasp and you drink
Then throw out my gloves
And throw on my mink

Born and Raised

I can find nothing better to do than strike a pen
Hoping to strike a match so we can start a fire
Racing the hands of the smothering man
I'm determined to get higher
I'm determined to inspire
In a toxic nation
Where we grow where we are planted
As if we have been stationed
And as of right now I have not chosen a destination
To infinity and beyond, I'm seeking intellect elevation
I just want to live through creation
And I am not talking about babies
If he asks me to marry him
I will have to speak in maybes
Because my ass would rather fall down in a Mercedes
Than be stuck on Medicaid, see
I have worked too hard to give it all up now
But I cannot see ahead of me
So I am still wondering how
I am going to beat the odds

Don't want to be a statistic
But I am struggling to stay above the law
And we all act so blessed, but bitch we ain't gifted
Worshipping many Gods
Just to get our spirits lifted
Doing many drugs
Smoking, drinking, and sniffing
File a police report
Amber Alert
All our morals missing
Can’t find love when you’re too busy dissing
Souls are almost extinct, same path as kissing
They don't hear me though
These motherfuckers won't listen
So full of shit that their eyes garbage glisten
Dumpsters for brains content in their positions
Kingdoms still reigned and they’re still just jesters
With as much rank as Wednesday's Uncle Fester
Grow up to be Chester the molesters
But these weak-minded bastards
Preach life could be lesser
Slept their whole life on the floor without a bed
Can’t help their children with homework
Because they have been misled
They don’t know shit because they’re not well-read
Won't write on their headstone
They were stoned in the head

Never forgotten is what they said

But what was his name again? What was his mark?

Did he lend his last name to a park?

Or did he miss his start?

His fire never sparked

Light My Fire

If I Ever Get Around to Living

The only thing I'm worried about running empty is my pen. Need a sponsorship with BIC to last me 'til the end. I could write the game; Watch me write my win. Lead is my oil-- it's greater than gold to me. Some won't comprehend because they can't write phenomenally. I put the Lucy in fur-- the lady in mink. Spank me when I sin, but don't take away my ink. And like a submarine, I'm still swimming when I sink. It all started when I read The Diary of Anne Frank. Made me value stories and to her I do give thanks. **Helen Keller saw life's beauty and she didn't even have sight. Now there's some shit to lie down and think about at night**. Like Keri said sometimes love knocks you down, but she forgot to mention it will stomp you through the ground, steal your direction, and spin your ass around. Where is TomTom when you need him? He's always skipping town. That's why I don't want him; I just need a crowd. They say it takes a village to raise a child and I say I'm still waiting. A relationship with my parents I debated. They weren't dedicated. Or perhaps they were-- to self-medicating. Stepped on a dirty drug needle age four caught hepatitis. Started a campaign hoping people won't let that divide us. Kind of feel like Rosa sitting on the front of the bus, "You can touch me, it won't hurt you I promise!" Some call me a hero and some call me a whore. Some leave me alone and some come back for more. But it's hard to recognize your worth when you're scraping yourself off the floor.

Love is a Verb

I will "are you okay?" you to fucking death, I swear.

Delivered

Walt Grace's Submarine Test, January 1967

Am I strong enough?

To be strong for the both of us?

Whiskey, Whiskey, Whiskey

Now you got a flat, Jack
Pop the whip and push back
Grab your tools and Jack, Jack
Spirits low
Flow the coke and Jack, Jack
Should have had breakfast in bed

A Face to Call Home

I will never bring you water

When you are thirsting in our bed

I, too, understand dry-mouthedness

So I sympathize instead

Paradise Valley

Wildfire

Grizzly,

Be my bone crusher

Squeeze me until the love

Pops my eyes out of--

Disoriented

Coffin rented

Lay me

Dear Marie

Perfection is an illusion

Just like you and I--

And them, too

Waitin' on the Day

Clinging to a magic eight ball

Patiently awaitin' waitin'

Shaking shaking shaking shaking

For the right display and

I'm up all night

Just writing writing writing

It shows dedication

Thoughts running running running

I might need medication

The more I know

The less I grow

They call it education

Mind trapped in devastation

Someone is watching

They call it investigation

Throw me behind bars

I call it paid vacation

You think we are free

We are strictly regulated

Culturally separated

Social-class segregation

Enlightenment regression
I call it humanity degradation
I'm just sa-sa-sa-sa-saying
Clinging to a magic eight ball
Patiently awaitin' waitin'
Shaking shaking shaking shaking

Paper Doll

My mother threatened to down a prescription bot-
tle standing over my father

Then my beau's ex-wife threatened to kill their daughter

And told the judge that I might try to harm her

Call Me the Breeze

From this time today
To this time tomorrow
My thoughts are consumed
With dreams of love and sorrow
I lost the ability to pray
When words became my ammo
Sitting next to Hemingway
And we're shooting at swallows
So, I don't aim at deities
I merely marvel my hollow
Existing on the energy
Of the mysteries we follow

Who You Love

Because I wonder

I wonder, I wonder

I do

I catch myself thinking about you

And I wonder if you think about me too

Because I wonder

I wonder, I wonder

Was it magic?

Was the energy between us

Always making static?

I wonder

I Will Be Found (Lost at Sea)

All the fish in the sea don't matter
If you are longing for a lion.

You're No One 'Til Someone Lets You Down

If Kanye West could hear me
I know that he would feel me
Emotionally not literally
Figuratively he would come into me
He would see me
He would be me
Immensely and infinitely
Plotting and planning and creating
And achieving and receiving much scrutiny
They watch for our fall
They are all deceiving
Living with a lack of meaning
Demeanors demeaning
And I cannot hear you over their/there screaming
Because my ear is numb to the world
And I am believing I am not a human being
If Kanye West could hear me
I know that he would feel me
Emotionally not literally

Figuratively he would come into me

He would see me

He would be me

Immensely and infinitely

Badge and Gun

Fort Knox. Like Fort Knox
Heart in an icebox
Little Red Riding the Charlie Foxtrot
Whispering, pulling your locks
I only say 'I love you' as I'm kissing on your balls
You are hard as cement
Like these million goddamn walls
Guarded

On the Way Home

Mama thinks I'd be a good lawyer
Because I've mastered the art of defending
Witnessed too much rule-bending
Maybe I should be an actress
Because I've mastered the art of pretending
I agree with what you say
Because your opinions are never-ending
So instead of advice-lending
I'm just practicing blending into the situation
I know that I'm the factor
That determines if this equation
Is a negative or a positive
I'm rearranging my feelings
No ego dedication
It's up to me to hold it together or cause devastation
So instead of retaliation, I send my mind on vacation
I take one to the dome to destination unknown
When I'm lost in the trees, that's when I feel at home

The Search for Everything

Still Feel Like Your Man

Do you remember that night
When we were on the phone
You had gone to The London
You were there all alone
You called me and said baby
I'm about to fuck this hoe
Call me in the morning
To make sure I made it home
Did you still feel like my man
As you folded her over the dresser
Did it break your heart when
I folded under the pressure?

Emoji of a Wave

Mixed emotions
Deep as the ocean
Locomotion
Love potion
Had me doting
Now I'm toting
The weight of your words
Like a shot to the head
Like I'm numb
Or we're dead
Murder-suicide
Triggered by your pride

Helpless

The haves and the have nots innit
Funny how the have nots get it
And the haves don't know the half of it
One percent don't know their staffs and shit
But they say slavery ended, didn't it
Meanwhile, majority of us are living it

Love on the Weekend

Tell me what is love? Is it a kiss? Is it a hug?
A fire of the soul or a friction burn from rug?
Show me a simple shrug
Because I know you don't know
I can see it in your boyish glow
Behind your curious eyes
Behind your tongue-tied lies
Between your heavily thrusting thighs
Baby, you are your own demise
Settling for what feels wrong
Because it looks good in a thong
Because her ideas are not too strong
And you know you won't be held down long
Hear me now as I wail out my song
That's veiled behind a sarong
Of everything you find pretty
Because love is so surreal
It doesn't mind stooping to petty
Getting sliced up by your machete of words
That you swear to be true
As they act as magic holding me together like glue

Oh, thank you
And on cue, you return to your wife
I'll be waiting for next Friday night

In the Blood

Family full of addicts
I'm dabbling in the industry
World full of savages
And it's doing something funny to me
Driving kilos across the country
Because there's nothing like the money to me
They say blood is thicker than water
But water nourishes the cemeteries
All my relatives done is make it harder for me
Always strung out, never sung out
They're killing, you see
Smoking, drinking, sniffing, and not caring about me
So I push the things that ended their dreams
Because they ripped my heart open at its seams
So it seems I'll be enabling instead of disabling genes
For neither of our benefit because they don't give a shit

Changing

Figments of you
In my imagination
I turn the dial
Change the station
I pour the vial
Chant incantations
Make you believe
Make believe you
Is your inclination

Theme from "The Search for Everything"

The read of your rhetoric
The silence in the spaces
I could never get ahead of it
You live steps ahead of my paces
Maybe it's the way you always make me chase
Or the idea of the enchanted place
That lingers behind your face
The music in your fingertips
The mystery on your lips
Or the promise of your absence
Because I am afraid to commit

Moving On and Getting Over

Attention, retention, detention, suspension
Reminiscing, dismissing, missing, now kissing
Then dissing, pitching fitting, re-emitting
Technology and time, drop of dimes, in they chime
Heart jittery throbbing, apple bottom bobbing
Drooling while they're fooling, big icy jewelry
Now in remission, seems I'm lacking vision
Peaking at our pictures, seeking your attention

Never on the Day You Leave

Slick like honey
When I'm getting money
There is no tension, fuck a pension
I make my own decisions
No rubber-- no revisions
Gone are your visions
When my metal erases your senses
So don't act senseless
Just please don't do it
I would hate to see your family in church
Carrying you through it
And who it?
I didn't do it
Prove it

Rosie

If the pink streaks are where Venus meets Apollo,
Then paint me into your sheets like Picasso.

Roll it on Home

Rose in the East, but I'm headed West, raise me
Like a poker game when the players all betraying
They don't think I'm serious
But I tell them I'm not playing
They'll be on their knees tonight
There's no debating
Then for fellating and again for sacred praying
You can say I'm wrong for that
But hell, I'm just saying
Go repent on Sunday
And hit the plate to pay in
Then worry about making rent
For the place you stay in

You're Gonna Live Forever in Me

And when the current sways in the other direction
I'll carry you in my reflection looking back at me
I hope you see you are a part of my identity

Thou
Shalt
Not
Falter
at
My
Alter

I Guess I Just Feel Like

Muse me if you must
I can't even muster the courage to bust your soul's lust
Let your brain nut, sexually abuse me in the butt
Rape me of my dignity
Water down my sanity as you watch me rust
Drowning for your love
While you're pleading to come into me
But you refuse to cum into me
You don't understand what that does to me mentally
I would do anything for you to see me
More than just your inspiration creatively
I want you to create with me
I want you to call it destiny
I want you to relate to me
I want to give you the best of me
I want you to create with me
I want to give you the rest of me

With Gratitude For

John Mayer, among many men

Don't say
"Hey There"
When you see me
with John Mayer

Made in the USA
Middletown, DE
24 November 2020

25068374R00059